Mastering 11+

CEM
Practice Papers
Book 1

ashkraft
EDUCATIONAL

Mastering 11+ © 2015 ashkraft educational

This page is intentionally left blank

Mastering 11+
CEM Exam Practice Papers
Book 1

Copyright © 2015 ASHKRAFT EDUCATIONAL

Mastering 11+ is a trade mark of ashkraft educational.

ASHKRAFT EDUCATIONAL HAS NO ASSOCIATION WITH
CEM, DURHAM UNIVERSITY, GL, ANY SCHOOL OR EXAMINATION BOARDS.

ISBN: 1910678171
ISBN-13: 978-1-910678176

9 781910 678176

"Practice is everything.
This is often misquoted as Practice makes perfect"

Table of Contents

PRACTICE PAPER – 1

This paper has two parts of 45 minutes each.

PART - A

Maximum time allowed: 45 minutes

CEM Eleven Plus Exam

Paper 1 – Part A

INSTRUCTIONS:

- **Do not turn this page until you are told to do so.**

- **Read the instructions at the beginning of every section carefully. Mark your answers neatly using a horizontal line on the answer sheet.**

- **Each section is timed. When you finish a section, wait until you are told to move onto the next section.**

- **If you make a mistake, rub it out and mark your new answer clearly.**

- **You will have a total of 45 minutes for this part of the test.**

- **Any rough working should done on a separate piece of paper.**

- **Answer carefully, but as quickly as you can.**

SECTION 1: Select the word that has the same or closest meaning to the primary word on the left. There is only one correct answer for each question.

Mark your selection on the answer sheet.   Maximum time allowed: 5 Minutes

Question Number	Primary Word	Options				
		A	B	C	D	E
1	**VANQUISHER**	Conqueror	Forgotten	Dud	Disappear	Underdog
2	**OPAQUE**	Transparent	Visible	Dense	Translucent	Clear
3	**STEADFAST**	Speedy	Firm	Wavering	Indecisive	Shaky
4	**COURTEOUS**	Impolite	Boorish	Courtyard	Bold	Considerate
5	**RAMPANT**	Contained	Wild	Upstream	Included	Trifling
6	**TEMPERATE**	Moderate	Hot	Extreme	Severe	Acute
7	**ELEGANT**	Ragged	Grungy	Refined	Unkempt	Shabby
8	**FORSAKEN**	Forgiven	Abandoned	Reserved	Restrained	Forgetful
9	**VACATE**	Trip	Holiday	Evacuate	Plug	Block
10	**PIOUS**	Sincere	Immoral	Irreverent	Phased	Ungodly
11	**INNOCUOUS**	Innocent	Offensive	Nasty	Invasive	Belligerent
12	**EVADE**	Duck	Confront	Face	Encounter	Defy
13	**SUMPTUOUS**	Meagre	Mean	Inadequate	Paltry	Lavish
14	**WEIGHT**	Burden	Hold	Grace	Agility	Nimble
15	**EXPEDITE**	Impede	Accelerate	Inhibit	Hamper	Block

Mastering 11+ / CEM Exam Practice

SECTION 2: Read the poetry below carefully and then answer the questions that follow. For each question record your answer on the answer sheet by choosing one of the options.

Maximum time allowed: 15 Minutes

The Wreck of the Hesperus

It was the schooner Hesperus,
That sailed the wintry sea;
And the skipper had taken his little daughter,
To bear him company.

Blue were her eyes as the fairy-flax,
Her cheeks like the dawn of day,
And her bosom white as the hawthorn buds,
That ope in the month of May.

The skipper he stood beside the helm,
His pipe was in his mouth,
And he watched how the veering flaw did blow
The smoke now West, now South.

Then up and spake an old Sailòr,
Had sailed to the Spanish Main,
"I pray thee, put into yonder port,
For I fear a hurricane.

"Last night, the moon had a golden ring,
And to-night no moon we see!"
The skipper, he blew a whiff from his pipe,
And a scornful laugh laughed he.

Colder and louder blew the wind,
A gale from the Northeast,
The snow fell hissing in the brine,
And the billows frothed like yeast.

Down came the storm, and smote amain
The vessel in its strength;
She shuddered and paused, like a frighted steed,
Then leaped her cable's length.

He wrapped her warm in his seaman's coat
Against the stinging blast;
He cut a rope from a broken spar,
And bound her to the mast.

"O father! I hear the church-bells ring,
Oh say, what may it be?"
"'T is a fog-bell on a rock-bound coast!"—
And he steered for the open sea.

"O father! I hear the sound of guns,
Oh say, what may it be?"
"Some ship in distress, that cannot live
In such an angry sea!"

"O father! I see a gleaming light,
Oh say, what may it be?"
But the father answered never a word,
A frozen corpse was he.

Lashed to the helm, all stiff and stark,
With his face turned to the skies,
The lantern gleamed through the gleaming snow
On his fixed and glassy eyes.

Then the maiden clasped her hands and prayed
That saved she might be;
And she thought of Christ, who stilled the wave,
On the Lake of Galilee.

And fast through the midnight dark and drear,
Through the whistling sleet and snow,
Like a sheeted ghost, the vessel swept
Tow'rds the reef of Norman's Woe.

And ever the fitful gusts between
A sound came from the land;
It was the sound of the trampling surf
On the rocks and the hard sea-sand.

"Come hither! Come hither! My little daughter,
And do not tremble so;
For I can weather the roughest gale
That ever wind did blow."

16	What do you think is a schooner?

A. Yacht
B. Perfectionist
C. Flawed
D. Ill Fated

17	Who did the skipper have for company?

A. His daughter
B. A Spaniard
C. Hesperus
D. Fairy Flax

18	Which of the following best describes the skipper's daughter?

A. Ugly duckling
B. Captain's lucky charm
C. A pretty young girl
D. Puzzled

19	What was the old sailor's request to the Captain?

- A. To not to take him sailing
- B. Not to see the moon with a golden ring
- C. To visit the markets on the port
- D. To dock the ship on a port as he feared there to be a hurricane

20	What made the old sailor to place such a request?

- A. He was scared of hurricanes
- B. It was bad luck to see the moon with a golden ring
- C. The markets on the port were cheap
- D. Seeing the moon with a golden ring the last night and not seeing a moon tonight

21	How did the captain react to the old sailor's request?

- A. He believed the sailor and granted his wish
- B. He laughed and ignored him
- C. He was fuming at such a silly request
- D. He asked his daughter to fulfil the old sailor's wish

22	Why did the Captain tie his daughter to the mast?

- A. To stop her from leaving his ship
- B. To protect her from the severe weather
- C. To protect her from the evil old sailor
- D. None of the above

23	Why did the Captain stop answering his distressed daughter's questions?

- A. He was busy steering the ship away from the coast
- B. He was busy cutting the rope from a broken spar
- C. He had frozen to death
- D. He was busy saving the sailor

24 **Why did the little girl think of the Christ?**

    A.   To pray that she be saved from the hurricane
    B.   To pray that her father be returned
    C.   To wonder how he might have calmed the waves
    D.   To pray that the sailor be saved

25 **Where does the ship end up?**

    A.   Deep into the bottom of the ocean
    B.   Lake of Galilee
    C.   Reef of Norman's Woe
    D.   Became a lost ghost ship

SECTION 3: Work out and select ONE correct answer for each of the short maths questions below. Mark your answer on the answer sheet.

Maximum time allowed: 10 Minutes

26	How many hours are there in a week?					
	A	B	C	D	E	F
	168	164	24	158	178	174

27	What is 40% of £13,000?					
	A	B	C	D	E	F
	£520	£52	£5200	£4200	£6300	£630

28	What is $^1/_{10}{}^{th}$ of a litre?					
	A	B	C	D	E	F
	100 l	10 ml	100 ml	250 ml	1 ml	1.0 ml

29	What is the radius of a circle with diameter of 12.50 cm?					
	A	B	C	D	E	F
	6.25 ml	62.5 cm	6.25cm	6.25mm	6.25 m	625mm

30	A coach is travelling at a speed of 95 km per hour. What distance will it travel in 3.5 hours?					
	A	B	C	D	E	F
	33.25 km	332.5 km	332.5m	3.25km	232.25km	242.25km

31	What is the perimeter of a square whose area is 625 cm² ?					
	A	B	C	D	E	F
	25 cm	2.5 cm	2.5 mm	15 cm	100 cm	22.5 cm

32	Which of the following is a square number?					
	A	B	C	D	E	F
	2	8	15	25	35	44

33 What is the value of the equation below, if "x" is 3 and "y" is 5?

$$2x^3 + 5y^2$$

A	B	C	D	E	F
179	189	169	159	149	241

34 What is the next number in the sequence below?

1   4   3   16   5   36   7

A	B	C	D	E	F
57	58	64	8	9	56

35 The ratio of boys to girl at a local school is 3:4.
The number of boys in the school are 270.
What is the total number of students at the school?

A	B	C	D	E	F
360	630	410	415	770	800

36 How many edges does a triangular prism have?

A	B	C	D	E	F
3	6	8	9	12	16

37 What is the square root of 256?

A	B	C	D	E	F
13	14	15	16	17	18

38 What is the remainder you get when you divide 22 by 7?

A	B	C	D	E	F
1	2	3.14	3	4	3.1

39 A train reaches its destination after travelling 50 minutes at 10:15 AM.
What time did the journey start?

A	B	C	D	E	F
9:30 AM	9:25 AM	9:25 PM	9:30 PM	9:20 AM	10:25 AM

40	What is $\dfrac{3.5 \times 3 + 2.5 \times 3}{4 \times 0 + 1.5 \times 2}$?					
	A	B	C	D	E	F
	3	6	12	2.57	5.14	1.0

SECTION 4: NON-VERBAL REASONING

Instructions: Find the next shape in the sequence.

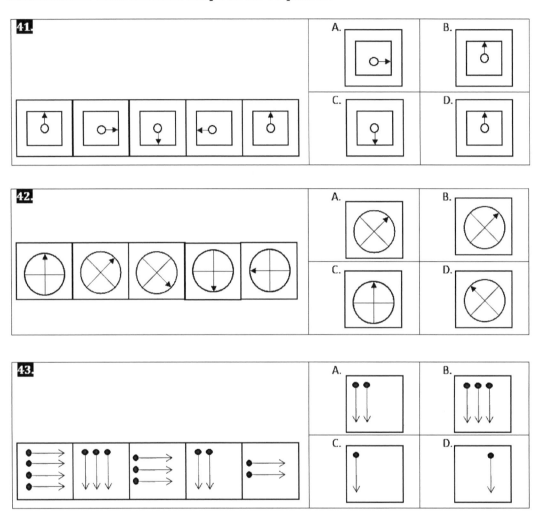

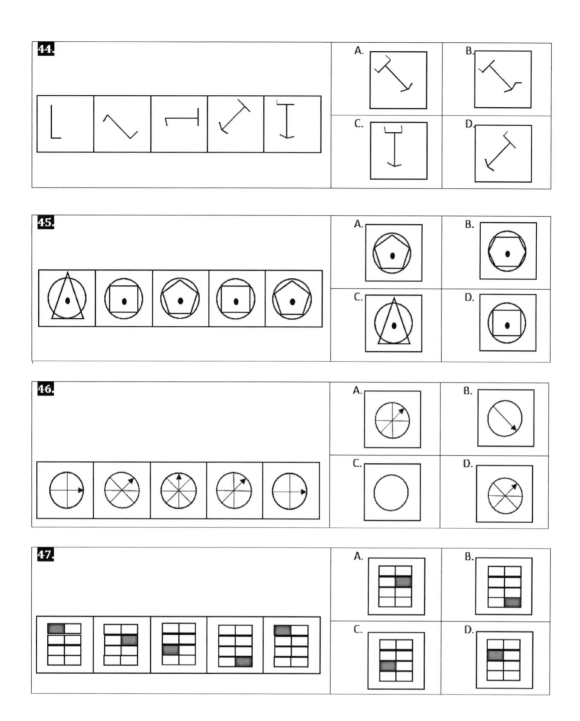

Instructions:

The two shapes on the left have been added/merged together. Choose what the result will look like from the options on the right.

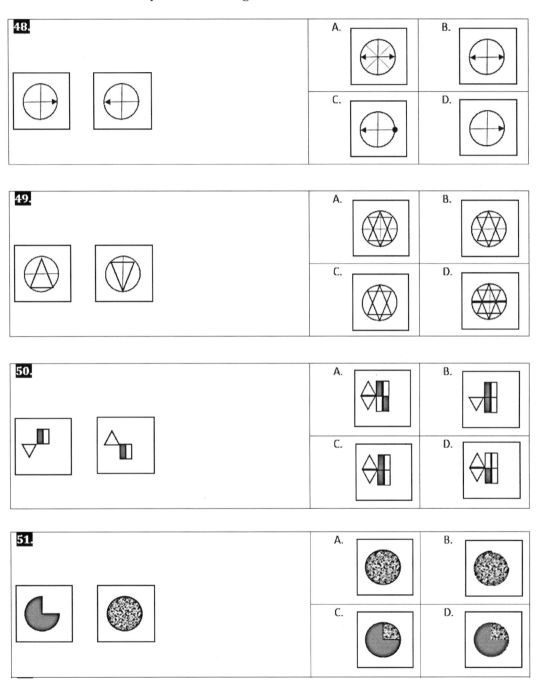

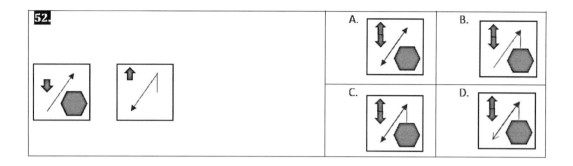

Instructions:

In each of these questions compare the figure in the first box with the figure in the second box. Then look at the figure in the third box and find its partner in the boxes on the right.

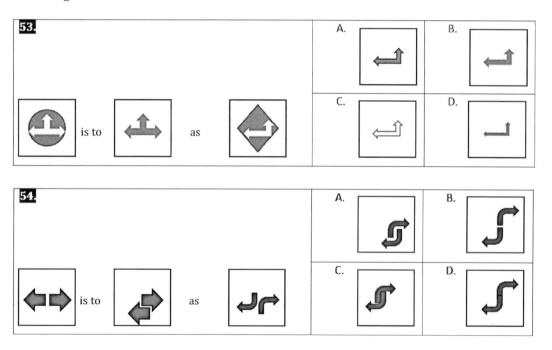

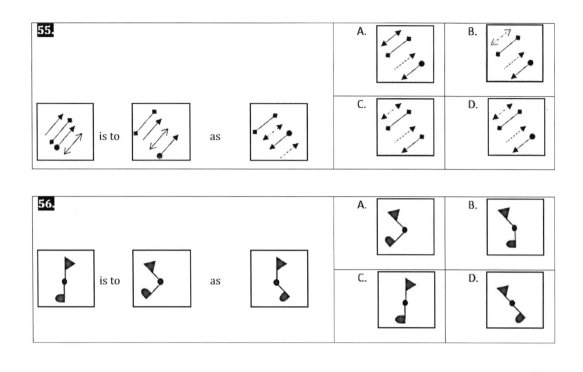

Instructions:

There are five patterns with each pattern representing two letters at the edge of each box. Work out the missing two letter code for the last box.

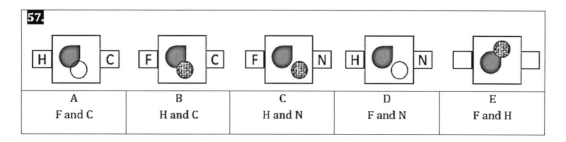

A	B	C	D	E
F and C	H and C	H and N	F and N	F and H

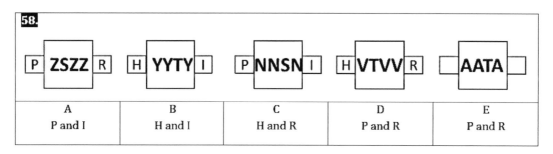

A	B	C	D	E
P and I	H and I	H and R	P and R	P and R

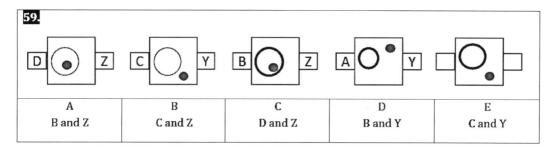

A	B	C	D	E
B and Z	C and Z	D and Z	B and Y	C and Y

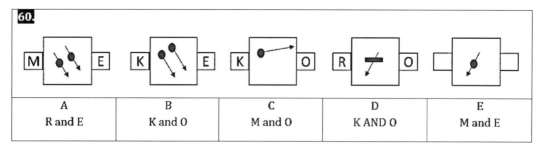

A	B	C	D	E
R and E	K and O	M and O	K AND O	M and E

You have finished the first part of the exam paper.

You are advised to take a 15 minutes break before you start Part – B.

PART - B

Maximum time allowed: 45 minutes

CEM Eleven Plus Exam

Paper 1 – Part B

INSTRUCTIONS:

- Do not turn this page until you are told to do so.

- Read the instructions at the beginning of every section carefully. Mark your answers neatly using a horizontal line on the answer sheet.

- Each section is timed. When you finish a section, wait until you are told to move onto the next section.

- If you make a mistake, rub it out and mark your new answer clearly.

- You will have a total of 45 minutes for this part of the test.

- Any rough working should done on a separate piece of paper.

- Answer carefully, but as quickly as you can.

SECTION 1: Select the word that has the **opposite meaning** to the primary word on the left. There is **only one correct answer** for each question.

Mark your selection on the answer sheet.   Maximum time allowed: 5 Minutes

Question Number	Primary Word	Options				
		A	B	C	D	E
1	**JADED**	Exhausted	Bored	Weary	Cynical	Fresh
2	**PROFICIENT**	Incompetent	Skilled	Capable	Skilful	Adept
3	**WICKED**	Unimpressive	Impressive	Fantastic	Fabulous	Terrific
4	**ESTEEM**	Respect	Contempt	Honour	Value	Icy
5	**EXASPERATE**	Placate	Rile	Enrage	Frustrate	Rotate
6	**SECONDARY**	Ancillary	Derived	Consequent	Primary	Tributary
7	**VINTAGE**	Essential	Traditional	Prime	Atypical	Pure
8	**STRICKEN**	Well	Suffering	Distracted	Suffering	Wracked
9	**VIRTUAL**	Simulated	Essential	Implicit	Real	Cybernetic
10	**TOXIC**	Deadly	Weapon	Armed	Harmless	Venomous
11	**ARCTIC**	Frozen	Bitter	Tropical	Frigid	Temperate
12	**INTERNAL**	External	Centre	Core	Domestic	Centric
13	**DIMINISH**	Dwindle	Lessen	Consolidate	Weaken	Deteriorate
14	**SWAGGER**	Coyness	Arrogance	Bluster	Conceit	Boastfulness
15	**ENDANGERED**	Common	Threatened	Scarce	Rare	Vanishing

SECTION 2: For each question in the following passage, select the most appropriate word from the table below.

Mark your selection on the answer sheet.   Maximum time allowed: 5 Minutes

A. conversation	B. heart	C. mischief	D. resolute	E. whether

On the evening of Fan's visit, Polly sat down before her fire with a [**16**] and

thoughtful aspect. She pulled her hair down, turned her skirt back, put her feet on the

fender, and took Puttel into her lap, all of which arrangements signified that something

very important had got to be thought over and settled. Polly did not soliloquize aloud,

as heroines on the stage and in books have a way of doing, but the

[**17**] she held with herself was very much like this: "I'm afraid there

is something in it. I've tried to think it's nothing but vanity or imagination, yet I can't

help seeing a difference, and feeling as if I ought not to pretend that I don't. I know it 's

considered proper for girls to shut their eyes and let things come to a crisis no matter

how much [**18**] is done. But I don't think it 's doing as we 'd be done

by, and it seems a great deal more honest to show a man that you don't love him before

he has entirely lost his [**19**] . The girls laughed at me when I said so,

and they declared that it would be a very improper thing to do, but I 've observed that they don't hesitate to snub 'ineligible parties,' as they call poor, very young, or

unpopular men. It 's all right then, but when a nice person comes it 's part of the fun to

let him go on to the very end, **20** [   ] the girls care for him or not.

SECTION 3: For each question in the following passage, select the most appropriate word from the options given.

Mark your selection on the answer sheet   Maximum time allowed: 10 Minutes

Santa Claus lives in the Laughing Valley, where stands the big, rambling castle in which

his toys are **21**

A	▭	destroyed
B	▭	alive
C	▭	manufactured

. His workmen, selected from the ryls,

knooks, pixies and fairies, live with him, and every one is as busy as can be from one

year's end to another.

It is called the Laughing Valley because everything there is **22**

A	▭	toy
B	▭	happy
C	▭	ryls

and gay. The brook chuckles to itself as it leaps rollicking between its green banks; the

wind whistles merrily in the trees; the sunbeams dance lightly over the soft grass, and

the violets and wild flowers look smilingly up from their green nests. To laugh one needs

to be happy; to be happy one needs to be **23**

A	▭	content
B	▭	rich
C	▭	happy

.   And

throughout the Laughing Valley of Santa Claus contentment reigns supreme.

On one side is the mighty Forest of Burzee. At the other side stands the huge mountain

that contains the Caves of the Daemons. And between them the Valley lies smiling and

peaceful.

One would think that our good old Santa Claus, who **24**
- A ▭ wastes
- B ▭ devotes his
- C ▭ ravages

days to making children happy, would have no enemies on all the earth; and, as a matter

of fact, for a long period of time he encountered nothing but love wherever he might go.

But the Daemons who live in the mountain caves **25**
- A ▭ lived
- B ▭ grew to
- C ▭ desperate

hate Santa Claus very much, and all for the simple reason that he made children happy.

The Caves of the Daemons are five in number. A broad pathway leads up to the first cave,

which is a finely arched cavern at the **26**
- A ▭ feet
- B ▭ mouth of the mountain, the
- C ▭ foot

entrance being beautifully carved and decorated. In it resides the Daemon of

Selfishness. Back of this is another cavern inhabited by the Daemon of Envy. The cave of the Daemon of Hatred is next in order, and through this one passes to the home of the

Daemon of Malice—situated in a **27**
- A ☐ **bright**
- B ☐ **lovely**
- C ☐ **dark**

and fearful cave in the

very heart of the mountain. I do not know what lies beyond this. Some say there are

terrible pitfalls leading to death and destruction, and this may very well be true.

However, from each one of the four caves mentioned there is a small,

28
- A ☐ **narrow**
- B ☐ **wide**
- C ☐ **large**

tunnel leading to the fifth cave—a cozy little room

occupied by the Daemon of Repentance. And as the rocky floors of these passages are

well worn by the track of passing feet, I judge that many wanderers in the Caves of the

Daemons have **29**
- A ☐ **died**
- B ☐ **escaped**
- C ☐ **evidenced**

through the tunnels to the abode of the

Daemon of Repentance, who is said to be a pleasant sort of fellow who gladly opens for

one a little door **30**
- A ☐ **admitting**
- B ☐ **admiring**
- C ☐ **abolishing**

you into fresh air and sunshine

again.

SECTION 4: Select TWO words from the each group of words that does not belong to that group.

Mark your selections on the answer sheet.   Maximum time allowed: 5 Minutes

Question Number	A	B	C	D	E
31	Hazy	Vibrant	Foggy	Clear	Blurred
32	Earth	Soil	Dirt	Grit	Pebble
33	Compassion	Sympathy	Malice	Clemency	Brutality
34	Kitten	Dog	Pup	Calf	Boar
35	Virtuous	Malevolent	Perfect	Immoral	Pious
36	Pen	Scalpel	Blade	Pencil	Stiletto
37	Roof	Window	Door	Carpet	Rug
38	Violet	Indigo	Blue	Black	White
39	Penne	Fusilli	Pasta	Macaroni	Noodles
40	Sturdy	Weak	Strong	Rickety	Secure
41	Livid	Furious	Mad	Shriek	Holler
42	Lamb	Chicken	Beef	Duck	Turkey
43	Wasteful	Immoderate	Excessive	Thrifty	Frugal
44	Tatters	Assets	Scraps	Treasures	Rags
45	Soup	Meat	Bisque	Vegetables	Broth

SECTION 5: The table below lists the answers for the questions in this exercise in a random order. Match the correct answers to each question.

Mark your selections on the answer sheet.   Maximum time allowed: 10 Minutes

A	B	C	D	E
8	25.40	10 cm	-18	£2.23
F	G	H	I	J
25	9	£6500	20	£43750

46	What is the height of a triangle whose area is 50 cm² and the base is 10 cm?
47	A cab can carry five passengers. How many cabs are required to carry 42 people?
48	What is half of 50.80?
49	How many days are there between 28th September and 5th October, both inclusive?
50	What is the square root of 625?
51	How many 250ml bottles can be filled with 5 litres of orange juice?
52	Monica puts aside 5% of her earnings into a savings account for a rainy day. Her current annual salary is £65,000. How much money would she have saved in two years?
53	What is **6 x 12 / (6 - 10)** ?

54	Rob has £20 and spends £17.77 in a shop. How much money is remaining?
55	What is 35% of £125,000?

SECTION 6: Work out and mark your answers by filling the appropriate grids on the answer sheet. Use a separate sheet for your working.

Maximum time allowed: 15 minutes

> *The circumference of a circle is calculated using the formula 2 ∏ r, where ∏ is 3.14 and "r" is the radius.*
>
> *The area of a circle is calculated using the formula ∏ r^2*
> *An inch is the same as 2.54 cm.*
>
> *Use these facts and formulae to answer the following questions.*

56	The approximate radius of the London eye big wheel is 68 meters. What is the circumference rounded to the nearest meter?
57	If the wheel were to be unraveled it is believed it will be 1.5 times longer than one of the tallest building in London. How tall is the building being compared to, rounded to the nearest meter?
58	What is the distance travelled if the wheel revolved 50 times? Round your answer to the nearest kilometer.
59	What is the area of the big wheel, rounded to the nearest unit?
60	The wheel has 32 capsules and can carry 800 people in total per revolution. What is the average number of people per capsule?

END OF PART - B

You have finished the second and final part of the exam paper 1.

This completes Practice Paper 1.

ANSWER SHEET

PRACTICE PAPER - ONE

ashkraft
EDUCATIONAL

NAME: _____

REGISTRATION ID: _____

DATE:

CEM Style Test Practice
Paper 1 - Part A
ANSWER SHEET

SECTION 1	SECTION 2

SECTION 1

1. A B C D E
2. A B C D E
3. A B C D E
4. A B C D E
5. A B C D E
6. A B C D E
7. A B C D E
8. A B C D E
9. A B C D E
10. A B C D E
11. A B C D E
12. A B C D E
13. A B C D E
14. A B C D E
15. A B C D E

SECTION 2

16. A B C D
17. A B C D
18. A B C D
19. A B C D
20. A B C D
21. A B C D
22. A B C D
23. A B C D
24. A B C D
25. A B C D

SECTION 3

26	A	B	C	D	E	F
27	A	B	C	D	E	F
28	A	B	C	D	E	F
29	A	B	C	D	E	F
30	A	B	C	D	E	F
31	A	B	C	D	E	F
32	A	B	C	D	E	F
33	A	B	C	D	E	F
34	A	B	C	D	E	F
35	A	B	C	D	E	F
36	A	B	C	D	E	F
37	A	B	C	D	E	F
38	A	B	C	D	E	F
39	A	B	C	D	E	F
40	A	B	C	D	E	F

SECTION 4

41	A	B	C	D
42	A	B	C	D
43	A	B	C	D
44	A	B	C	D
45	A	B	C	D
46	A	B	C	D
47	A	B	C	D
48	A	B	C	D
49	A	B	C	D
50	A	B	C	D
51	A	B	C	D
52	A	B	C	D
53	A	B	C	D
54	A	B	C	D
55	A	B	C	D
56	A	B	C	D
57	A	B	C	D
58	A	B	C	D
59	A	B	C	D
60	A	B	C	D

SECTION 1

	A	B	C	D	E
1	A	B	C	D	E
2	A	B	C	D	E
3	A	B	C	D	E
4	A	B	C	D	E
5	A	B	C	D	E
6	A	B	C	D	E
7	A	B	C	D	E
8	A	B	C	D	E
9	A	B	C	D	E
10	A	B	C	D	E
11	A	B	C	D	E
12	A	B	C	D	E
13	A	B	C	D	E
14	A	B	C	D	E
15	A	B	C	D	E

SECTION 2

	A	B	C	D	E
16	A	B	C	D	E
17	A	B	C	D	E
18	A	B	C	D	E
19	A	B	C	D	E
20	A	B	C	D	E

SECTION 3

	A	B	C
21	A	B	C
22	A	B	C
23	A	B	C
24	A	B	C
25	A	B	C
26	A	B	C
27	A	B	C
28	A	B	C
29	A	B	C
30	A	B	C

	SECTION 4							SECTION 5									
31	A	B	C	D	E		**46**	A	B	C	D	E	F	G	H	I	J
32	A	B	C	D	E		**47**	A	B	C	D	E	F	G	H	I	J
33	A	B	C	D	E		**48**	A	B	C	D	E	F	G	H	I	J
34	A	B	C	D	E		**49**	A	B	C	D	E	F	G	H	I	J
35	A	B	C	D	E		**50**	A	B	C	D	E	F	G	H	I	J
36	A	B	C	D	E		**51**	A	B	C	D	E	F	G	H	I	J
37	A	B	C	D	E		**52**	A	B	C	D	E	F	G	H	I	J
38	A	B	C	D	E		**53**	A	B	C	D	E	F	G	H	I	J
39	A	B	C	D	E		**54**	A	B	C	D	E	F	G	H	I	J
40	A	B	C	D	E		**55**	A	B	C	D	E	F	G	H	I	J
41	A	B	C	D	E												
42	A	B	C	D	E												
43	A	B	C	D	E												
44	A	B	C	D	E												
45	A	B	C	D	E												

Mastering 11+ / CEM Exam Practice

SECTION 6:

Question Number	Answer Grid	Question Number	Answer Grid
56	0 0 0 0 0 1 1 1 1 1 2 2 2 2 2 3 3 3 3 3 4 4 4 4 4 5 5 5 5 5 6 6 6 6 6 7 7 7 7 7 8 8 8 8 8 9 9 9 9 9	**59**	0 0 0 0 0 1 1 1 1 1 2 2 2 2 2 3 3 3 3 3 4 4 4 4 4 5 5 5 5 5 6 6 6 6 6 7 7 7 7 7 8 8 8 8 8 9 9 9 9 9
57	0 0 0 0 0 1 1 1 1 1 2 2 2 2 2 3 3 3 3 3 4 4 4 4 4 5 5 5 5 5 6 6 6 6 6 7 7 7 7 7 8 8 8 8 8 9 9 9 9 9	**60**	0 0 0 0 0 1 1 1 1 1 2 2 2 2 2 3 3 3 3 3 4 4 4 4 4 5 5 5 5 5 6 6 6 6 6 7 7 7 7 7 8 8 8 8 8 9 9 9 9 9
58	0 0 0 0 0 1 1 1 1 1 2 2 2 2 2 3 3 3 3 3 4 4 4 4 4 5 5 5 5 5 6 6 6 6 6 7 7 7 7 7 8 8 8 8 8 9 9 9 9 9		

PRACTICE PAPER – 2

This paper has two parts of 45 minutes each.

PART - A

Maximum time allowed: 45 minutes

CEM Eleven Plus Exam

Paper 2 – Part A

INSTRUCTIONS:

- Do not turn this page until you are told to do so.

- Read the instructions at the beginning of every section carefully. Mark your answers neatly using a horizontal line on the answer sheet.

- Each section is timed. When you finish a section, wait until you are told to move onto the next section.

- If you make a mistake, rub it out and mark your new answer clearly.

- You will have a total of 45 minutes for this part of the test.

- Any rough working should done on a separate piece of paper.

- Answer carefully, but as quickly as you can.

SECTION 1: Select the word that has the same or closest meaning to the primary word on the left. There is only one correct answer for each question.

Mark your selection on the answer sheet.   Maximum time allowed: 5 Minutes

Question Number	Primary Word	Options				
		A	B	C	D	E
1	**SOVEREIGN**	Superior	Dependent	Partial	Biased	Restricted
2	**REBELLIOUS**	Stubborn	Yielding	Amenable	Compatible	Religious
3	**TRANSFIGURE**	Maintain	Convert	Preserve	Continue	Sustain
4	**ADJUDICATE**	Arbitrate	Arbitrage	Mesmerist	Entertain	Amend
5	**STAGNATE**	Invent	Renew	Originate	Transform	Fester
6	**FAMINE**	Female	Plenty	Abundance	Glut	Shortage
7	**STRIKE**	Formal	Attack	Action	Activity	Lack
8	**SUSTAIN**	Withstand	Clasp	Close	Collapse	Crumple
9	**MINT**	Used	Leaf	New	Ancient	Pittance
10	**PROVIDENT**	Wasteful	Profligate	Prudent	Rash	Extravagant
11	**SHEATH**	Icy	Covering	Plenty	Group	Jungle
12	**MINGLE**	Mix	Arrive	Drink	Feeble	Meek
13	**CASTING**	Irritate	Shadow	Meadow	Molding	Job
14	**INTERROGATE**	Entrance	Interim	Grill	Stable	Unstable
15	**FUNDAMENTAL**	Superfluous	Central	Redundant	Needless	Spare

Mastering 11+ / CEM Exam Practice

SECTION 2: Read the passage below carefully and then answer the questions that follow. For each question record your answer on the answer sheet by choosing one of the options.

Maximum time allowed: 15 Minutes

When Mary Lennox was sent to Misselthwaite Manor to live with her uncle everybody said she was the most disagreeable-looking child ever seen. It was true, too. She had a little thin face and a little thin body, thin light hair and a sour expression. Her hair was yellow, and her face was yellow because she had been born in India and had always been ill in one way or another. Her father had held a position under the English Government and had always been busy and ill himself, and her mother had been a great beauty who cared only to go to parties and amuse herself with happy people. She had not wanted a little girl at all, and when Mary was born she handed her over to the care of an Ayah, who was made to understand that if she wished to please the Mem Sahib she must keep the child out of sight as much as possible. So when she was a sickly, fretful, ugly little baby she was kept out of the way, and when she became a sickly, fretful, toddling thing she was kept out of the way also. She never remembered seeing familiarly anything but the faces of her Ayah and the other native servants, and as they always obeyed her and gave her her own way in everything, because the Mem Sahib would be angry if she was disturbed by her crying, by the time she was six years old she was as tyrannical and selfish a little pig as ever lived. The young English governess who came to teach her to read and write disliked her so much that she gave up her place in three months, and when other governesses came to try to fill it they always went away in a shorter time than the first one. So if Mary had not chosen to really want to know how to read books she would never have learned her letters at all.

One frightfully hot morning, when she was about nine years old, she awakened feeling very cross, and she became crosser still when she saw that the servant who stood by her bedside was not her Ayah.

"Why did you come?" she said to the strange woman. "I will not let you stay. Send my Ayah to me."

The woman looked frightened, but she only stammered that the Ayah could not come and when Mary threw herself into a passion and beat and kicked her, she looked only more frightened and repeated that it was not possible for the Ayah to come to Missie Sahib.

There was something mysterious in the air that morning. Nothing was done in its regular order and several of the native servants seemed missing, while those whom Mary saw slunk or hurried about with ashy and scared faces. But no one would tell her anything and her Ayah did not come. She was actually left alone as the morning went on, and at last she wandered out into the garden and began to play by herself under a tree near the veranda when she heard her mother come out on the veranda with someone. She was with a fair young man and they stood talking together in low strange voices. Mary knew the fair young man who looked like a boy. She had heard that he was a very young officer who had just come from England. The child stared at him, but she stared most at her mother. She always did this when she had a chance to see her, because the Mem Sahib—Mary used to call her that oftener than anything else—was such a tall, slim, pretty person and wore such lovely clothes. Her hair was like curly silk and she had a delicate little nose which seemed to be disdaining things, and she had large laughing eyes. All her clothes were thin and floating, and Mary said they were "full of lace." They looked fuller of lace than ever this morning, but her eyes were not laughing at all. They were large and scared and lifted imploringly to the fair boy officer's face.

"Is it so very bad? Oh, is it?" Mary heard her say.

"Awfully," the young man answered in a trembling voice. "Awfully, Mrs. Lennox. You ought to have gone to the hills two weeks ago."

The Mem Sahib wrung her hands.

"Oh, I know I ought!" she cried. "I only stayed to go to that silly dinner party. What a fool I was!"

At that very moment such a loud sound of wailing broke out from the servants' quarters that she clutched the young man's arm, and Mary stood shivering from head to foot. The wailing grew wilder and wilder. "What is it? What is it?" Mrs. Lennox gasped.

"Someone has died," answered the boy officer. "You did not say it had broken out among your servants."

"I did not know!" the Mem Sahib cried. "Come with me! Come with me!" and she turned and ran into the house.

After that, appalling things happened, and the mysteriousness of the morning was explained to Mary. The cholera had broken out in its most fatal form and people were dying like flies. The Ayah had been taken ill in the night, and it was because she had just died that the servants had wailed in the huts. Before the next day three other servants were dead and others had run away in terror. There was panic on every side, and dying people in all the bungalows.

During the confusion and bewilderment of the second day Mary hid herself in the nursery and was forgotten by everyone. Nobody thought of her, nobody wanted her, and strange things happened of which she knew nothing. Mary alternately cried and slept through the hours. She only knew that people were ill and that she heard mysterious and frightening sounds. Once she crept into the dining-room and found it empty, though a partly finished meal was on the table and chairs and plates looked as if they had been hastily pushed back when the diners rose suddenly for some reason. The child ate some fruit and biscuits, and being thirsty she drank a glass of wine which stood nearly filled. It was sweet, and she did not know how strong it was. Very soon it made her intensely drowsy, and she went back to her nursery and shut herself in again, frightened by cries she heard in the huts and by the hurrying sound of feet. The wine made her so sleepy that she could scarcely keep her eyes open and she lay down on her bed and knew nothing more for a long time.

Many things happened during the hours in which she slept so heavily, but she was not disturbed by the wails and the sound of things being carried in and out of the bungalow.

16 **Why was Mary's face yellow?**

    A. Because she was born in India

    B. Because she was always ill

    C. Because she was looked after by an Ayah

    D. Because her father was always ill and yellow

17 **Why did the servants always obey Mary?**

    A. They did not want Mary to cry and disturb Mem Sahib

    B. Because they loved and respected her

    C. Because she was Missie Sahib

    D. It was a sign of respect for her parents

18 **What kind of a person Mary was by the time she was six?**

    A. A kind and polite child with good manners

    B. An intelligent child that could read and write

    C. Overbearing and selfish little girl

    D. Yellow and merciful

19 **What made Mary eventually learn the letters?**

    A. The fear of Mem Sahib

    B. The love of Ayah and other native servants

    C. Mary wanted to know how to read books

    D. The young English governess made her learn the letters

20 **Who was the fair young man in conversation with Mary's mother?**

    A. Mem Sahib

    B. Ayah

    C. Servant who came in place of Ayah

    D. A young officer from England

21 | **Why did the servants wail in their huts?**

    A. Because Ayah had died
    B. Because Mary had kicked the new servant
    C. Because Ayah was ill
    D. Because they did not like the young officer from England

22 | **What was the name of the fatal disease that killed Ayah?**

    A. Cholera
    B. Fever
    C. Yellow Fever
    D. A mysterious disease

23 | **What made Mary fall asleep for a long time?**

    A. She was ill
    B. Partly finished meal found in the kitchen which she ate
    C. The glass of wine she had
    D. She was tired of the mayhem going around her

24 | **How did Mary address her mother often?**

    A. Mrs. Lennox
    B. Ayah
    C. Missi Sahib
    D. Mem Sahib

25 | **Mrs. Lennox was sorry that she did not leave to the hills before the disease broke out. Why did she not go to the hills?**

    A. Because her servants were dying
    B. She stayed back to attend a dinner party
    C. Because she was a fool
    D. She stayed back to be with Mary as Ayah was not well

SECTION 3: Work out and select ONE correct answer for each of the short maths questions below.

Mark your answer on the answer sheet.　　　　　　　Maximum time allowed: 10 Minutes

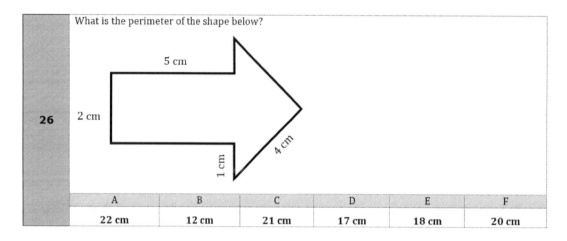

26	What is the perimeter of the shape below?					
	A	B	C	D	E	F
	22 cm	12 cm	21 cm	17 cm	18 cm	20 cm

27	Which of the following is a straight angle?					
	A	B	C	D	E	F
	45°	90°	135°	180°	270°	360°

28	What is $3/4^{th}$ of a km?					
	A	B	C	D	E	F
	250 m	500 m	750 m	850 m	1.75 km	225 m

29	What is the difference between 0.35 and 0.025?					
	A	B	C	D	E	F
	0.325	0.330	0.320	0.321	0.3215	0.291

30	What is the maximum individual angle in an equilateral triangle?					
	A	B	C	D	E	F
	45°	90°	60°	125°	100°	180°

31	What is the length of a square whose area is 400 cm²?					
	A	B	C	D	E	F
	80 cm	100 cm	20 cm	25 cm	50 cm	75 cm

32	Which of the following is a triangular number?					
	A	B	C	D	E	F
	1	5	9	10	16	27

33	What is the value of the equation below, if "x" is 3 and "y" is 0? $x^3 - 3y^2$					
	A	B	C	D	E	F
	27	24	18	9	18	21

34	What is 65% of £6,500?					
	A	B	C	D	E	F
	£5000	£4225	£5500	£5225	£5220	£4000

35	What is the cube root of 64?					
	A	B	C	D	E	F
	8	4	2	10	12	14

36	What is the next number in the sequence below? 1 4 3 6 5 8 7					
	A	B	C	D	E	F
	10	9	11	8	10	12

37	A local shop made £312.50 last Sunday by selling newspapers each priced at £1.25. How many newspapers were sold that day?					
	A	B	C	D	E	F
	25	100	175	200	225	250

38	Find the value of the following equation where "x" is 3 and "y" is 1. $\sqrt{2x^3 - 5y^2}$					
	A	B	C	D	E	F
	54	49	13	18	8	7

39	A sprinter runs 100m in 15 seconds. What is the speed of this performance expressed as km per hour?					
	A	B	C	D	E	F
	100 km/h	1 km/h	10 km/h	100 km/h	2.4 km/h	24 km/h

40	The minimum temperature today is 5°C less than yesterday which was recorded to be -2°C. What is today's temperature?					
	A	B	C	D	E	F
	7°C	-7°C	-3°C	-2°C	-1°C	-4°C

SECTION 4: In the questions below find **TWO words**, **one from EACH GROUP**, that are **similar** in meaning and mark them using the appropriate letter on the answer sheet.

Maximum time allowed: 3 Minutes

Question Number	GROUP ONE			GROUP TWO		
	A	**B**	**C**	**D**	**E**	**F**
41	Agile	Gawky	Bungling	Clumsy	Inept	Lively
42	Universal	Temperate	Joinery	Connect	Woodcraft	Unite
43	Enemy	Alien	Foe	Foreigner	Ally	Friend
44	Singular	Plenty	Quite	Odd	Thrifty	Sparing
45	Splendid	Witch	Craft	Wizard	Awesome	Genius

SECTION 5: In the questions below find **TWO words, one from EACH GROUP**, that are **opposite** in meaning and mark them using the appropriate letter on the answer sheet.

Maximum time allowed: 4 Minutes

Question Number	GROUP ONE			GROUP TWO		
	A	**B**	**C**	**D**	**E**	**F**
46	Tentative	Fidelity	Surplus	Uncertain	Assured	Hesitant
47	Justify	Defensive	Swagger	Aggressive	Apologetic	Cautious
48	Apart	Jaded	Switch	Plenty	Surplus	Together
49	Defeat	Success	Economy	Grandeur	Clarity	Gentle
50	Bowl	Flimsy	Catch	Durable	Match	Chase

SECTION 6: NON-VERBAL REASONING

Instructions: Find the next shape in the sequence.

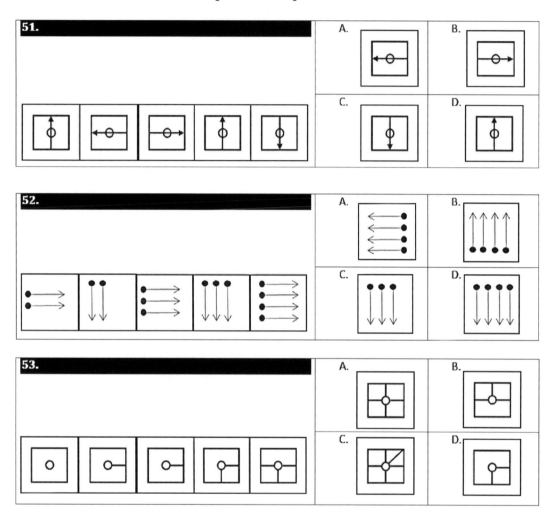

Instructions: Find the MISSING shape in the sequence.

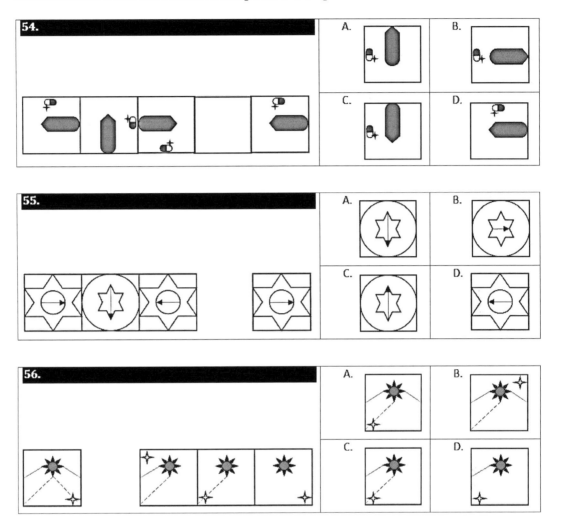

Instructions:

The two shapes on the left have been added/merged together. Choose what the result will look like from the options on the right.

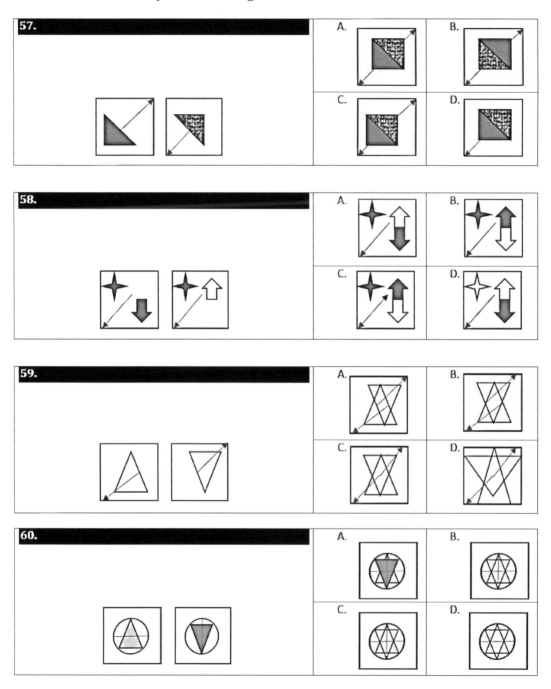

END OF PART - A

You have finished the first part of the exam paper.

You are advised to take a 15 minutes break before you start Part – B.

PART - B

Maximum time allowed: 45 minutes

CEM Eleven Plus Exam

Paper 2 – Part B

INSTRUCTIONS:

- Do not turn this page until you are told to do so.

- Read the instructions at the beginning of every section carefully. Mark your answers neatly using a horizontal line on the answer sheet.

- Each section is timed. When you finish a section, wait until you are told to move onto the next section.

- If you make a mistake, rub it out and mark your new answer clearly.

- You will have a total of 45 minutes for this part of the test.

- Any rough working should done on a separate piece of paper.

- Answer carefully, but as quickly as you can.

SECTION 1: Select the word that has the opposite meaning to the primary word on the left. There is only one correct answer for each question.

Mark your selection on the answer sheet.   Maximum time allowed: 5 Minutes

Question Number	Primary Word	Options				
		A	B	C	D	E
1	ESOTERIC	Mysterious	Abstruse	Cryptic	Frank	Occult
2	ORTHODOX	Revolutionary	Conformist	Conventional	Approved	Established
3	CRUCIAL	Trivial	Imperative	Vital	Critical	Essential
4	COINCIDE	Concur	Correspond	Differ	Agree	Match
5	QUEASY	Well	Easy	Woozy	Nauseous	Unsettled
6	IMPOSING	Striking	Stately	Daunting	Grand	Mediocre
7	ASPIRATIONAL	Unambitious	Motivated	Ambitious	Hopeful	Thrusting
8	SEPERATION	Division	Multiplication	Partition	Unification	Universal
9	THRIVE	Flourish	Fail	Boom	Blossom	Grow
10	APPRECIATE	Gain	Grow	Escalate	Depreciate	Value
11	GENERAL	Common	Typical	Technical	Broad	Vague
12	PROLIFERATE	Grow	Dwindle	Prosper	Multiply	Replicate
13	LETDOWN	Success	Failure	Descent	Comedown	Go Up
14	LUMINOUS	Glowing	Grey	Shining	Gleaming	Shimmering
15	DETACH	Attach	Isolate	Remove	Separate	Disengage

SECTION 2: For each question in the following passage, select the most appropriate word from the table below.

Mark your selection on the answer sheet   Maximum time allowed: 5 Minutes

A. remembered	B. computation	C. address	D. inhabitants	E. manners

Two Donkeys and the Geese lived on the Green, and all other residents of any social standing lived in houses round it. The houses had no names. Everybody's

16 [_____] was, "The Green," but the Postman and the people of the place

knew where each family lived. As to the rest of the world, what has one to do with the

rest of the world, when he is safe at home on his own Goose Green? Moreover, if a

stranger did come on any lawful business, he might ask his way at the shop.

Most of the **17** [_____] were long-lived, early deaths being exceptional; and

most of the old people were proud of their age, especially the sexton, who would be

ninety-nine come Martinmas, and whose father **18** [_____] a man who had

carried arrows, as a boy, for the battle of Flodden Field. The Grey Goose and the big Miss

Jessamine were the only elderly persons who kept their ages secret. Indeed, Miss

Jessamine never mentioned any one's age, or recalled the exact year in which anything

had happened. She said that she had been taught that it was bad **19** [_____]

to do so "in a mixed assembly."

The Grey Goose also avoided dates, but this was partly because her brain, though intelligent, was not mathematical, and [**20**] was beyond her. She never got farther than "last Michaelmas," "the Michaelmas before that," and "the Michaelmas before the Michaelmas before that." After this her head, which was small, became confused, and she said, "Ga, ga!" and changed the subject.

SECTION 3: For each question in the following passage, select the most appropriate word from the options given.

Mark your selection on the answer sheet.   Maximum time allowed: 10 Minutes

But she remembered the little Miss Jessamine, the Miss Jessamine with the "conspicuous" hair. Her aunt, the big Miss Jessamine, said it was her only fault. The hair was clean, was abundant, was glossy, but do what you would with it, it never looked like other people's. And at church, after Saturday night's wash, it shone like the best brass

fender after a **㉑** A ▭ **spring**
            B ▭ **gentle**
            C ▭ **pristine**

cleaning. In short, it was conspicuous, which does not become a young woman—especially in church.

Those were worrying times altogether, and the Green was used for strange purposes. A political meeting was held on it with the village Cobbler in the **㉒** A ▭ **chair**
            B ▭ **house**
            C ▭ **pond**

and a speaker who came by stage coach from the town, where they had wrecked the bakers' shops, and discussed the price of bread. He came a second time, by stage, but the people had heard something about him in the meanwhile, and they did not keep him on the Green. They took him to the pond and tried to make him swim, which he could not do, and the whole affair was very

23
- A ☐ soothing
- B ☐ reassuring
- C ☐ disturbing

to all quiet and

peaceable fowls. After which another man came, and preached sermons on the Green,

and a great many people went to hear him; for those were "trying times," and folk ran

hither and thither for comfort. And then what did they do but drill the ploughboys on

the Green, to get them ready to fight the French, and teach them the goose-step!

However, that **24**
- A ☐ went
- B ☐ reached
- C ☐ came

to an end at last, for Bony was sent to St.

Helena, and the ploughboys were sent back to the plough.

Everybody lived in fear of Bony in those days, especially the naughty children, who were

kept in order during the day by threats of, "Bony shall have you," and who had

25
- A ☐ dreams
- B ☐ nightmares
- C ☐ visions

about him in the dark. They thought he was an Ogre in

a cocked hat. The Grey Goose thought he was a fox, and that all the men of England were

going out in red coats to hunt him. It was no use to argue the point, for she had a very

small head, and when one idea got into it there was no **26**
- A ☐ room
- B ☐ time
- C ☐ roam

for another.

Besides, the Grey Goose never saw Bony, nor did the children, which rather spoilt the

terror of him, so that the Black Captain became more effective as a Bogy with hardened

offenders. The Grey Goose remembered his coming to the place perfectly. What he came

for she did not pretend to know. It was all part and parcel of the war and bad times. He

was called the Black Captain, **27**
A ▭ **paltry**
B ▭ **mainly** because of himself, and
C ▭ **partly**

partly because of his wonderful black mare. Strange stories were afloat of how far and

how fast that mare could go, when her master's hand was on her mane and he

28
A ▭ **bellowed**
B ▭ **whispered** in her ear. Indeed, some people thought we might
C ▭ **screeched**

reckon ourselves very lucky if we were not out of the frying-pan into the fire, and had

not got a certain well-known Gentleman of the Road to protect us against the French.

But that, of course, made him none the less useful to the Johnson's Nurse, when the little

Miss Johnsons were naughty.

"You leave off crying this minnit, Miss Jane, or I'll give you right away to that horrid

wicked officer. Jemima! just look out o' the windy, if you please, and see if the Black

Cap'n's a-com-ing with his horse to carry away Miss Jane."

And there, sure enough, the Black Captain strode by, with his 29

A	☐	swagger
B	☐	eyes
C	☐	sword

clattering as if it did not know whose head to cut off first. But he did not call for Miss

Jane that time. He went on to the Green, where he came so suddenly upon the eldest

Master Johnson, sitting in a puddle on purpose, in his new nankeen skeleton suit, that

the young gentleman thought judgment had overtaken him at last, and abandoned

himself to the howlings of 30

A	☐	despair
B	☐	bliss
C	☐	delight

.

SECTION 4: Select TWO words from the each group of words that does not belong to that group.

Mark your selections on the answer sheet.   Maximum time allowed: 5 Minutes

Question Number	A	B	C	D	E
31	Sun	Venus	Moon	Jupiter	Earth
32	Shirt	Jacket	Shoe	Trouser	Slipper
33	Clock	Microscope	Watch	Timer	Chronology
34	Partial	Fractional	Limited	Extensive	Full
35	Rainbow	Colour	Violet	Indigo	Blue
36	Isolate	Embrace	Detach	Include	Contain
37	Gold	Silver	Platinum	Metal	Jubilee
38	Strength	Flaw	Fault	Drawback	Robustness
39	Vision	Night	Sleep	Hallucination	Dream
40	Caught	Taught	Drop	Strike	Spent
41	Tennis	Football	Racquet	Bat	Golf
42	England	Canada	Germany	Brazil	France
43	Cowardly	Brave	Heroic	Plucky	Craven
44	Stealth	Honesty	Secrecy	Openness	Covertness
45	Leap	Drop	Drib	Jump	Spike

SECTION 5: The table below lists the answers for the questions in this exercise in a random order. Match the correct answers to each question.

Mark your selections on the answer sheet.   Maximum time allowed: 10 Minutes

A	B	C	D	E
4.7	21	7	45	120
F	G	H	I	J
250	15	120	1600	12

46	What is $^3/_4$th of £160?
47	One mile is the same as 1.6 km. How many meters in a mile?
48	The temperature in London is 3°C and the temperature in Birmingham is -4°C. Find the difference between the two.
49	What is **5.5 – 0.8?**
50	What is the square root of 225?
51	What is the perimeter of a hexagon whose sides are 2 cm in length?
52	The total cost of a pilgrimage is £480. Robert has deposited 75% of the cost with the tour operator. What is the balance amount he needs to pay?
53	How many days are in three weeks?

54	There are 128 cars parked in a car park with room for another 122. What is the maximum capacity of the car park?
55	Luke is 32 years old. Waseem is 13 years older. How old is Waseem?

SECTION 6: Work out and mark your answers by filling the appropriate grids on the answer sheet. Use a separate sheet for your workings.

Maximum time allowed: 10 minutes

> *Daniel heads up a global company manufacturing mobile phones and earns an annual salary of £150,000.*
>
> *The tax on this income is charged as per the rules below:*
> - *No tax on the first £10,000*
> - *20% tax on income between £10,001 and £40,000*
> - *40% tax on income above £40,000*

56	How much tax will Daniel pay in a year, rounded to the nearest ten pound?
57	How much money does Daniel gets paid after tax, every year? Round it to the nearest ten pound.
58	If Daniel also received a bonus of £55,000 and benefits worth £15,000 how much more tax he will have to pay that year? Round it to the nearest ten.
59	Express the bonus as a percentage of his basic salary. Round it to the nearest unit.
60	Daniel is putting 10% of his annual salary into a pension fund. What is the total amount of pension savings in a year?

END OF PART - B

You have finished the second and final part of the exam paper 2.

This completes Practice Paper 2.

ANSWER SHEET

PRACTICE PAPER - TWO

ashkraft
EDUCATIONAL

You can download additional copies of the answer sheet from
www.mastering11plus.com

NAME: _____

REGISTRATION ID: _____

DATE:

CEM Style Test Practice
Paper 2 - Part A
ANSWER SHEET

SECTION 1						SECTION 2			
1	A	B	C	D	E	16	A	B	C	D
2	A	B	C	D	E	17	A	B	C	D
3	A	B	C	D	E	18	A	B	C	D
4	A	B	C	D	E	19	A	B	C	D
5	A	B	C	D	E	20	A	B	C	D
6	A	B	C	D	E	21	A	B	C	D
7	A	B	C	D	E	22	A	B	C	D
8	A	B	C	D	E	23	A	B	C	D
9	A	B	C	D	E	24	A	B	C	D
10	A	B	C	D	E	25	A	B	C	D
11	A	B	C	D	E					
12	A	B	C	D	E					
13	A	B	C	D	E					
14	A	B	C	D	E					
15	A	B	C	D	E					

SECTION 3							SECTION 4 & 5					
26	A	B	C	D	E	F	41	A	B	C	D	E	F
27	A	B	C	D	E	F	42	A	B	C	D	E	F
28	A	B	C	D	E	F	43	A	B	C	D	E	F
29	A	B	C	D	E	F	44	A	B	C	D	E	F
30	A	B	C	D	E	F	45	A	B	C	D	E	F
31	A	B	C	D	E	F	46	A	B	C	D	E	F
32	A	B	C	D	E	F	47	A	B	C	D	E	F
33	A	B	C	D	E	F	48	A	B	C	D	E	F
34	A	B	C	D	E	F	49	A	B	C	D	E	F
35	A	B	C	D	E	F	50	A	B	C	D	E	F
36	A	B	C	D	E	F	SECTION 6				
37	A	B	C	D	E	F	51	A	B	C	D
38	A	B	C	D	E	F	52	A	B	C	D
39	A	B	C	D	E	F	53	A	B	C	D
40	A	B	C	D	E	F	54	A	B	C	D
							55	A	B	C	D
							56	A	B	C	D
							57	A	B	C	D
							58	A	B	C	D
							59	A	B	C	D
							60	A	B	C	D

SECTION 1						SECTION 2				
1	A	B	C	D	E	16	A	B	C	D	E
2	A	B	C	D	E	17	A	B	C	D	E
3	A	B	C	D	E	18	A	B	C	D	E
4	A	B	C	D	E	19	A	B	C	D	E
5	A	B	C	D	E	20	A	B	C	D	E
6	A	B	C	D	E						
7	A	B	C	D	E	SECTION 3					
8	A	B	C	D	E	21	A	B	C		
9	A	B	C	D	E	22	A	B	C		
10	A	B	C	D	E	23	A	B	C		
11	A	B	C	D	E	24	A	B	C		
12	A	B	C	D	E	25	A	B	C		
13	A	B	C	D	E	26	A	B	C		
14	A	B	C	D	E	27	A	B	C		
15	A	B	C	D	E	28	A	B	C		
						29	A	B	C		
						30	A	B	C		

SECTION 4					
31	A	B	C	D	E
32	A	B	C	D	E
33	A	B	C	D	E
34	A	B	C	D	E
35	A	B	C	D	E
36	A	B	C	D	E
37	A	B	C	D	E
38	A	B	C	D	E
39	A	B	C	D	E
40	A	B	C	D	E
41	A	B	C	D	E
42	A	B	C	D	E
43	A	B	C	D	E
44	A	B	C	D	E
45	A	B	C	D	E

SECTION 5									
46	A	B	C	D	E	F	G	H	I	J
47	A	B	C	D	E	F	G	H	I	J
48	A	B	C	D	E	F	G	H	I	J
49	A	B	C	D	E	F	G	H	I	J
50	A	B	C	D	E	F	G	H	I	J
51	A	B	C	D	E	F	G	H	I	J
52	A	B	C	D	E	F	G	H	I	J
53	A	B	C	D	E	F	G	H	I	J
54	A	B	C	D	E	F	G	H	I	J
55	A	B	C	D	E	F	G	H	I	J

SECTION 6:

Question Number	Answer Grid	Question Number	Answer Grid
56	⓪①②③④⑤⑥⑦⑧⑨ (×5)	**59**	⓪①②③④⑤⑥⑦⑧⑨ (×5)
57	⓪①②③④⑤⑥⑦⑧⑨ (×5)	**60**	⓪①②③④⑤⑥⑦⑧⑨ (×5)
58	⓪①②③④⑤⑥⑦⑧⑨ (×5)		

ANSWERS

CEM Style Test Practice
Paper 1 - Part A

ANSWERS

Question Number	Answer	Question Number	Answer	Question Number	Answer	Question Number	Answer
1	A	16	A	31	E	46	D
2	C	17	A	32	D	47	A
3	B	18	C	33	A	48	B
4	E	19	D	34	C	49	A
5	B	20	D	35	B	50	C
6	A	21	B	36	D	51	C
7	C	22	B	37	D	52	C
8	B	23	C	38	A	53	B
9	C	24	A	39	B	54	A
10	A	25	C	40	B	55	D
11	A	26	A	41	A	56	B
12	A	27	C	42	D	57	A
13	E	28	C	43	C	58	B
14	A	29	C	44	A	59	E
15	B	30	B	45	D	60	C

ashkraft EDUCATIONAL

Question Number	Answer	Question Number	Answer	Question Number	Answer	Question Number	Answer
1	E	16	D	31	B and D	46	C
2	A	17	A	32	D and E	47	G
3	A	18	C	33	C and E	48	B
4	B	19	B	34	B and E	49	A
5	A	20	E	35	B and D	50	F
6	D	21	C	36	A and D	51	I
7	D	22	B	37	D and E	52	H
8	A	23	A	38	D and E	53	D
9	D	24	B	39	C and E	54	E
10	D	25	B	40	B and D	55	J
11	C	26	C	41	D and E	56	457 m
12	A	27	C	42	A and C	57	285 m
13	C	28	A	43	D and E	58	21 km
14	A	29	B	44	B and D	59	14519 m^2
15	A	30	A	45	B and D	60	25

CEM Style Test Practice
Paper 2 - Part A
ANSWERS

www.mastering11plus.com © 2015, ashkraft educational

Question Number	Answer	Question Number	Answer	Question Number	Answer	Question Number	Answer
1	A	16	B	31	C	46	A and E
2	A	17	A	32	D	47	B and D
3	B	18	C	33	A	48	A and F
4	A	19	C	34	B	49	C and D
5	E	20	D	35	B	50	B and D
6	E	21	A	36	A	51	B
7	B	22	A	37	F	52	D
8	A	23	C	38	B	53	A
9	C	24	D	39	F	54	C
10	C	25	B	40	B	55	C
11	B	26	A	41	A and F	56	B
12	A	27	D	42	C and E	57	C
13	D	28	C	43	B and D	58	A
14	C	29	A	44	A and D	59	A
15	B	30	C	45	A and E	60	A

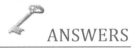
Question Number	Answer	Question Number	Answer	Question Number	Answer	Question Number	Answer
1	D	16	C	31	A and C	46	H
2	A	17	D	32	C and E	47	I
3	A	18	A	33	B and E	48	C
4	C	19	E	34	D and E	49	A
5	A	20	B	35	A and B	50	G
6	E	21	A	36	A and C	51	J
7	A	22	A	37	D and E	52	E
8	D	23	C	38	A and E	53	B
9	B	24	C	39	B and C	54	F
10	D	25	B	40	C and D	55	D
11	C	26	A	41	C and D	56	£50,000
12	B	27	C	42	B and D	57	£100,000
13	A	28	B	43	A and E	58	£28,000
14	B	29	C	44	B and D	59	37%
15	A	30	A	45	B and C	60	£15,000

If you need any clarification or explanation on any of the answers,
please drop us an email at

enquiry@mastering11plus.com

CEM books in the Mastering 11+ series:

- ➢ Mastering 11+ Vocabulary
- ➢ Mastering 11+ Synonyms and Antonyms

- ➢ English & Verbal Reasoning – Practice Book 1
- ➢ English & Verbal Reasoning – Practice Book 2
- ➢ English & Verbal Reasoning – Practice Book 3

- ➢ Cloze Tests – Practice Book 1
- ➢ Cloze Tests – Practice Book 2
- ➢ Cloze Tests – Practice Book 3

- ➢ Maths – Practice Book 1
- ➢ Maths – Practice Book 2
- ➢ Maths – Practice Book 3

- ➢ Comprehension – Multiple Choice Exercise Book 1
- ➢ Comprehension – Multiple Choice Exercise Book 2
- ➢ Comprehension – Multiple Choice Exercise Book 3

- ➢ CEM Practice Papers – Pack 1 (Papers 1 & 2)
- ➢ CEM Practice Papers – Pack 2 (Papers 3 & 4)
- ➢ CEM Practice Papers – Pack 3 (Papers 5 & 6)
- ➢ CEM Practice Papers – Pack 4 (Papers 7 & 8)

All queries to **enquiry@mastering11plus.com**

Printed in Great Britain
by Amazon